OXFORD
UNIVERSITY PRESS

My Week

Hayley Hetherington

On Monday, I went to school.

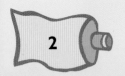

2

I listened to a story that the teacher read.
It was a good story.

Tuesday

On Tuesday, I went to school.

I read a story. The story was
about animals.

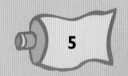

On Wednesday, I went to school.

I painted a picture. I painted the picture with my friends.

Thursday

On Thursday, I went to school.

8

I did some counting. I counted
to ten.

On Friday, I went to school.

I ate my lunch. I ate my lunch
with my friends.

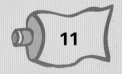

Saturday

On Saturday, I played football.

12

I played football with my brother.
I kicked the ball hard.

Sunday

On Sunday, I cleaned Mum's car.

14

I used lots of water. My brother used lots of water, too!

Monday	I listened to a story.	✓
Tuesday	I read a story.	✓
Wednesday	I painted a picture.	✓
Thursday	I did some counting.	✓
Friday	I ate my lunch.	✓
Saturday	I played football.	✓
Sunday	I cleaned Mum's car.	✓